First published in Italy
in 2010 by
Skira Editore S.p.A.
Palazzo Casati Stampa
via Torino 61
20123 Milano
Italy
www.skira.net

Printed and bound in Italy.
First edition

ISBN: 978-88-572-0782-7

Distributed in North America
by Rizzoli International Publications,
Inc., 300 Park Avenue South,
New York, NY 10010, USA.
Distributed elsewhere in the world
by Thames and Hudson Ltd.,
181A High Holborn, London WC1V 7QX,
United Kingdom.

Joachim Bessing

Franz Ferdinand

the tracht

SKIRA

In German-speaking countries, there is an item of clothing in the repertoire of men's wardrobe whose "reputation", "aura", or "effect" (however you might call it) is so misunderstood that at the mere mention of the word "Tracht" – or the naming of a specific part of this national costume, the "Janker"– an urbanite will wince, almost imperceptibly, but nonetheless as if he is terrified. Inwardly, the term "Tracht" unleashes a cascade of images: rows of folk music fans, their arms interlocked, drinking wine or beer from mugs that are far too large, and swaying this way and that to the rhythm of a brass band. This dance, performed while seated, is called "Schunkeln" and is part and parcel of the German "Gemütlichkeit". On such evenings, which, by the way, are still broadcast on television every now and then, your typical German or Austrian will appear dressed in a rustic outfit whose primary element is the traditional jacket: the "Trachtenjacke". The Oktoberfest in Munich, the "Wies'n", as it is called, has further contributed to some unfavourable associations with the jacket. Especially for young people as well as for the celebrities, who come to Munich from all over, this annual beer festival is a welcome opportunity to dress up in modernized versions of the national costume. During these weeks, the gossip columns in the daily papers and magazines are dominated by reports from the Oktoberfest. These supposedly famous faces, often flashed in unflattering poses ("schunkel"-ing along with their too-large mugs) are usually quickly forgotten. But the idea that the Tracht and tastelessness belong together perseveres.

Still, if one were to step aside and look for a moment, the jacket emerges as an attractive item of clothing – it is a classic. What's more, the Trachtenjacke, sometimes called a "Janker", along with the shirt with button facing and the straight-cut ankle-length pants, is essential to the overall outfit. **Its very name indicates its primary importance to the outfit and only a limited amount of variation is allowed** (and even then, each variation only accentuates the original form of the essential element). This somewhat abstract definition of tradition in fashion can be illustrated by the form of the lapel on a suit. The currently characteristic triangular incision (the "notch") at the level of the collarbone – they first came into fashion at the Congress of Vienna in the early nineteenth century and only a tailor would know what it's actually good for – is always present, even when a designer decides to have a suit made of laser beams, mirror shards, or rubber. Even, or rather, especially an outlandish, so-called avant-garde, design must bear the insignia of the original classic to heighten the contrast between its utopian vision and the background of tradition. Otherwise, it just hangs there in the air.

The insignia of the classic outfit is most obviously evident in the material of every Tracht jacket: the Loden is a felted woollen fabric, the manufacture of which will be later explored in detail. It is embroidered along the collar and, at times, also along the corners of the lapels or the ends of the sleeves. A special border is commonly used whose colour does not contrast with the fundamental tone of the Loden (I will have more to say about these ornamental braids as well). The jacket has one row of buttons. **Since it was originally a purely functional jacket, these**

buttons all the way up to the collar were important to protect the wearer's chest from cold, rain, or snow. In its classic form, the jacket has a narrow lapel, without the notch; each lapel on either side has one button. All the buttons on the jacket are made of either buckhorn or silver. Buckhorn is usually preferable because, **even today, deer have an almost cult-like status in some mountainous regions;** this surely has something to do with its appearance, its bizarre antlers. Like wildcats or colourfully feathered birds, deer are the kind of animal that people tend to view as civilized because they "present themselves" in fashionable attire. And even though the price of buckhorn is not noted on commodities markets, the material remains immeasurably valuable, above and beyond what it may be sold for, because, to this day, an inheritance law determines who may collect the antlers, called "Stangen" (sticks), and under what conditions, once they've been dropped. What normally happens is that the administrator of a hunting ground will present the owner with a selection so that he can choose the best pieces. If he has them made into buttons for his Tracht, **the lustrous aura of such buckhorn buttons outshines that of silver buttons, even those decorated with coats of arms.**

Traditionally, silver decorates women's Trachts in the Alpine regions. Around Bregenz, Austria, north of Lake Constance and far and away from Vienna, a woman can wear a Tracht that will take one's breath away, even today. The multi-part dress is made of jet-black lacquered material that – as with Mariano Fortuny and Issey Miyake – is folded into sharp plissés. Fine silver jewellery – chains and

coins – are worn over it. The only colour, an intense ultramarine, appears in the form of an ornamental braid.
Wearing the Tracht as fine clothing dates back to a time before the emergence of metro-sexual fashion. Yet, with a certain modesty, particular elements of design can also be found in men's Tracht jacket that are classic but also have a strain of modernity that never goes out of style; this applies above all to the cut.

We can assume that the Tracht jacket first appeared as a functional item of clothing back in the late Middle Ages, even though there is no particular evidence to verify this. Nonetheless, the construction of the Tracht jacket has retained a principle that – regardless of the form of the lapel – dramatically distinguishes it from the canon of menswear. In a contemporary sense, the jacket might be said to be under-designed, meaning that it is set on the shoulders from which it hangs down as if from a coat hanger over the upper body. An ideal chest disappears within it, but so does a rounder figure. The Tracht jacket (specifically the top-of-the-line model made of Loden material and not variations on the theme à la Country Style or Manor Chic) is, in all its unpretentiously straight-lined design and manufacture, the antidote to the folksy culture described earlier; the Tracht is the precursor of all reductionist fashion to follow.

Actually, **the combination of Loden and buckhorn gives the Tracht a touch of class and, outside of its Alpine home, even of the exotic as well.**

This is why Kenzo Takada had himself photographed for *Elle* in the 1980s wearing a honey-yellow Janker. Karl

Lagerfeld, too, went through a Tracht phase and, inspired by an exhibition of Habsburg Style at the Metropolitan Museum in New York (*Fashions of the Hapsburg Era: Austria–Hungary*, December 1979 – August 1980), Yves Saint Laurent presented stylized Tracht jackets in his very next collection. There are also the intriguingly conservative lapel-less jackets Pierre Cardin made for a group photo of the Beatles that make obvious reference to the style of the Tracht; this photo would become iconic.

We have to thank Baptist Josef Fabian Sebastian of Austria for the introduction of the functional jacket into fashion's repertoire. The member of the House of Habsburg dressed a line of archdukes and is known colloquially to this day as Archduke Johann. A yodeler was named after him, but it was primarily

his reputation as something of a dandy
that established his popularity. Born in
Florence at the end of the eighteenth
century, he was, like all dandies, a man
of many interests and much curiosity; the
natural sciences engaged him as much
as viniculture, the early industries that
were just then in their infancies, and of
course, hunting and mountain climbing.
This is why he is also credited with
the discovery of the Alpine functional
jacket as a Janker, an item of clothing
worthy of standing on its own; this is
perfectly understandable, considering
that he wanted to explore the Alpine
world in a manner befitting his status.
When he married a commoner in a
secret ceremony on 18 February 1829,
Johann found himself no longer in line
for the Habsburg crown, but this was not
a catastrophe for him because he was a
proud individual, one able to elegantly
extract himself from the strictures of

1 *The Austrian Emperor Franz Joseph wearing people's clothes at the party for his eightieth birthday, August 1910*

2 *Bone and horn ornaments and trinkets for Tyrolean jackets*

3

3 *A detail of the Tracht costume, the traditional Steirer loden jacket with embroidered lapels decorated with buckhorn buttons*

4 *The Duke of Windsor's Tyrolean suit, 1936. It comprises a grey loden jacket appliqued with bottle green oak leaves, horn buttons, green piping, grey silk twill lining; a matching bottle green backless waistcoat, loden trousers with green piped side seams*

4

the social order (this ability might serve as a neutral definition of the dandy). He concentrated on effecting change in the state of Styria, instigating economic and social reforms in the valleys and rugged mountains of the "Poorhouse of Austria". **From the Styrians he took on the so-called "Steirerrock", the national costume known today in the world of international fashion as the "Tyrolean jacket". It is a grey Loden jacket with dark green lapels** and is cut as described above. Archduke Johann was a good-looking man with a sharp, hawk-like profile. That he, as a fallen nobleman, would take on the rural Tracht lent the former functional jacket an aristocratic aura and made it accessible to the world of fashion. **Anyone invited to a hunting party or a wedding in the country today will see the**

dress code on the invitation: "Tuxedo/Tracht"; this equal treatment given to the Tracht and the tuxedo as passe-partout for men's evening dress may be chalked up to tradition rather than just rustic country living.

And, just as the tuxedo evolved from a sort of house coat with a velvet cord and a silken shawl collar to a standard of high society, so, too, has the Tracht developed from its medieval beginnings as a functional jacket all the way through to mass-produced versions made perhaps by Knize in Graben near Vienna, or perhaps made in Paris or Tokyo or anywhere there is a concentrated interest in fashion culture, always undergoing new refinements, so that it remains socially presentable to this day.

Even though **we can assume that the invention of Loden was purely accidental,** the entire career of the Tracht can be read in the material from which the jacket is cut. Let's conjure up a scene from the past: long ago when an Alpine man's woollen jacket became dirty, he submerged it in warm water to clean it and then stomped on it to squeeze the water out and dry it. According to the recent research, this would have been in practice as early as the eleventh century. Once the jacket had dried, the owner would realize that the water and drying treatment has given the fabric a dense stability. He would also note that it had a greater resistance to wind and that the cloth meshing had become less penetrable. Later, there would be experiments with boiling the cloth and the results would reveal an even more strongly matted, weather-resistant material. The demands made on clothing during this period had less to do with aesthetics or presentation than with practicality.

By purposefully matting woollen material, one could make it more weather-resistant, warm and almost waterproof. Residents of the outlying countryside could hardly ask for more from a jacket: Loden perfectly matched their needs.

Today, the manufacture of Loden is concentrated in the Austrian towns of Schladming and Mandling in Ennstal beneath Hoher Dachstein, the second-highest mountain in the Northern Limestone Alps. Loden-Steiner, a company located in Mandling, still uses the "Hammerwalke", a tool dating back to the late nineteenth century. This process might call to mind another maker of functional clothing, for example, Levi's jeans. In the 1970s, Levi's sold their traditional looms to Japan and now highly valuable denim materials

come from there. The industrialized
manufacture proceeds thusly: original
Tyrolean Loden consists of 80 percent
virgin wool and 20 percent alpaca,
though other woollen mixtures are
possible. Once the wool has been washed,
the fibres are combed out, and the
roving is produced. At the loom, a loose,
not yet impenetrable weave is woven
which is made denser on the threading-
loom and then, under the influence
of moisture and heat, turned to felt.
Once the material has undergone this
procedure, it has shrunk by 25 percent.
The cloth is then washed and dyed (the
original colour of the natural material
is a light grey, and so was the Styrian
jacket worn by Archduke Johann). Finally,
the material is "ausgeschärt", that is,
the longest of the fibres are all cut to a
single, uniform length. A Janker made
of Loden is lined, always cut at straight
angles and sports either a chinoise-like

standing collar (which would then make it a Salzburg Janker) or the narrow lapels described above (making it a Henndorf Janker). While neither type of Janker has a cut in the back, one naturally sees them in modern Tracht jackets that have been more or less internationalized. Wristbands with buttonholes appear on these now and then as well, even though they serve only as ornamentation on more traditional models. The modern Tracht jacket (again, linen or leather "Country Style" jackets are excluded from discussion here) closes the cut in the back with a dragoon and offers the chest area a bit more shape with the usual tailoring.

An item of clothing with such a history, such an unbroken line of tradition, is fated to become a vehicle for a post-modern fashion designer's imagination.

The Austrian Helmut Lang, who saw his
international breakthrough in the 1980s
(and whose voice is missed like no other
living designer's since his retirement in
2002), in his impressively conceptualized
collections worked from the very
beginning with well-defined quotations
from the Tracht's form and material.
Even so, these references were often
misinterpreted. Early on, there were
men's shirts with embroidered silken
borders running horizontally just above
the navel. Fashion critics saw in them a
minimalist reduction of a cummerbund;
though, interestingly, with the example
from the Bregenz region noted above in
mind, the decorative border appears to
be a reference to the Tracht. The same
goes for Lang's preference for the solid
materials he would use for his suits
that are reminiscent of Loden. The
photographer Elfie Semotan recalls that
there was even to have been an entire